Homes keep us

Homes Keep Us Warm

Homes Keep Us Warm

a building block book

Lee Sullivan Hill

Carolrhoda Books, Inc./Minneapolis

To my husband, Gary, my sons, Adam and Colin, and my cat, Molly, who make our home warm, wherever we live
—L. S. H.

The photographs in this book are reproduced through the courtesy of: © Bob Firth/Firth Photobank, front cover, pp. 6, 7, 15, 25; © Betty Crowell, back cover, p. 18; © Nada Pecnik/Visuals Unlimited, p. 1; © Budd Titlow/Visuals Unlimited, p. 2; © Stephen Graham Photography, pp. 5, 9, 16, 26; © Steven Ferry, pp. 8, 22; © Wolfgang Kaehler, pp. 10, 13, 19, 29; © D. Cavagnaro/Visuals Unlimited, p. 11; © Raymond Gehman/Corbis, p. 12; © Howard Ande, pp. 14, 21; © Nancy Clauss, p. 17; © Mark E. Gibson/Visuals Unlimited, pp. 20, 27; © David Hanover/Tony Stone Images, p. 23; © Steve Strickland/Visuals Unlimited, p. 24; © Betty Kubis/Root Resources, p. 28.

Carolrhoda Books, Inc.
A division of Lerner Publishing Group
241 First Avenue North
Minneapolis, Minnesota, 55401 U.S.A.

Website address: www.lernerbooks.com

Library of Congress Cataloging-in-Publication Data

Hill, Lee Sullivan.
    Homes keep us warm / Lee Sullivan Hill.
        p.   cm. — (A building block book)
    Includes index.
    Summary: A simple introduction to the variety and beauty of homes around the world.
        ISBN 1-57505-430-2
    1. Dwellings—Juvenile literature. [1. Dwellings. 2. Home.] I. Title. II. Series:
Hill, Lee Sullivan, 1958—Building block book.
NA7120.H754   2001
392.3'6—dc21   99-37391

Manufactured in the United States of America
1 2 3 4 5 6 – JR – 06 05 04 03 02 01

Supper simmers. Family calls. Home is the place where you belong.

Homes give us shelter from the weather.

They keep us cool in summer and warm in winter.

Homes keep us dry when rain pours down.
Ping, ping, ping. Rain hits a tin roof. It plays a
song that sounds like home.

Some old homes had just one room, called a keeping room. There, the family kept their belongings. They shared meals and read aloud by the fire at night.

You can find spaces like the old keeping rooms
in new homes, too. Living room, dining room,
and kitchen blend into one great room for a
family to share.

Around the world, many families live in one-room homes. Inuit live in tents made of animal skins when they hunt in the summer.

Kuna Indians live in one-room homes on islands in Panama. They gather leaves from coconut trees and weave them into roofs and walls.

Some families travel around in one-room homes on wheels. A trailer has fold-down beds and a tiny kitchen. You can store things in every nook and cranny.

A home fits the way a family lives. People who fish live by the water. Cambodian fishing families live *on* the water. Houseboats are their homes.

Farmers often live near their fields.
A farmhouse hugs the earth like a tree
with deep roots.

People who work in cities often choose homes near their jobs. In cities, homes squeeze close together. Row houses lean against each other. They share roofs, walls, and sidewalks.

Homes in suburbs have more space. They're close to city jobs, but not far from the country. Green grass and trees fill the yards in between the houses.

Deep woods surround a cabin in Minnesota.
Trees—cut into logs—make the walls. People
often use materials they find nearby when
building a home.

Stones for a home in Scotland came from the rocky fields just beyond the village walls.

Mud from the ground makes adobe homes
strong. Thick walls of baked mud block the heat
of summer.

Bricks for a house in Maryland came from clay
dug up nearby. The clay was made into blocks
and baked in a fire to make it strong.

Some homes are made of concrete and steel. Apartment houses tower over the city. Imagine all you could see from your window if you lived on the thirty-third floor!

Some homes are plain. And others are magical. Architects can turn homes into art.

Architects plan homes before they are built. First they ask questions: Where will the family cook? Where will they sleep? How will they heat the house in winter? Then architects draw plans on paper and with computers.

Builders use the plans to make houses.
Carpenters, plumbers, and electricians put
together the pieces. They turn piles of material
into a home.

Some people would rather live in an old home than a new one. They like wide wood floors and wavy window glass. Worn steps and shady trees make old houses as comfortable as faded jeans.

Old or new, all homes need constant care and cleaning. You could clean your room right now. (Maybe later?) Or you could paint a playhouse hidden in the trees.

When you grow up, you could be a painter and paint houses many colors. You could be an architect and plan new homes. Or you could be a carpenter and frame walls out of wood.

Homes give us shelter and keep us safe. They give us a place to eat and to sleep. Homes make our hearts ache when we go away. They make us happy when we come back to stay.

Heart and soul, homes keep us warm.

A Photo Index to the Homes in This Book

Cover This sturdy American farmhouse is built of brick. It is called a single-family home, since one family lives in the house.

Page 1 Dunguaire Castle in County Galway, Ireland, was built in the 1520s. The castle was once home to the O'Heyne, O'Shaughnessy, and Martyn clans.

Page 2 A chimney rises from the roof of this home from the 1700s in Massachusetts. Inside, the chimney widens to a massive brick structure. Fireplaces in every room once kept the home warm in winter.

Page 5 Many bungalows were built between the 1900s and 1930s. People could order the homes right from the Sears Catalog! Three thousand dollars would buy a complete home, but an indoor bathroom cost extra.

Page 6 Heavy snow cloaks this cabin in Yellowstone National Park, Wyoming. Snow on the roof can help keep a home warm.

Page 7 The porch of this home in northern Arkansas is a nice place for a rocking chair on a rainy day. A porch is great on sunny days, too, creating shade and drawing cool air into the house.

Page 8 The Quarry Bank Mill Museum in Wilmslow, England, is a restored cotton mill and home. This room is part of the miller's house.

Page 9 This home in Dearborn, Michigan, was built in the 1960s and updated in the 1990s. The desire to gather around the hearth is just as strong as it was hundreds of years ago.

Page 10 Traditional Inuit families travel during the summer hunting season. This temporary hunting camp is on Southampton Island in Nunavut, Canada.

Page 11 A Kuna Indian repairs his home on the San Blas Islands in Panama. The process of weaving grasses or leaves between wooden supports is called thatching.

 **Page 12** A hitch at the front of this trailer connects it to a car or truck for traveling. Some people live year-round in trailers. Others use them for cross-country vacations.

 **Page 13** This houseboat is part of a floating village on a lake in Cambodia called Tonle Sap. The name Tonle Sap means "great lake." It is the largest lake in Southeast Asia.

 **Page 14** This farm is located just outside Kennard, Nebraska. When the farmhouse was built, new trees were planted to block fierce winter winds. Over the years, the trees have grown taller than the house!

 **Page 15** Row houses share walls because land costs so much in big cities. Small trees and bushes often decorate the front yards. Many row houses also have yards in back with flower or vegetable gardens.

 **Page 16** A few small trees have been planted beside this new home in a suburb of Ann Arbor, Michigan. How long do you think it will be before the trees grow taller than the house?

 **Page 17** Trees for a log cabin are cut into logs, the round edges shaved flat, and the ends notched. Then the logs must air-dry for at least six months before they can be stacked into walls.

 **Page 18** The Scottish stonemasons who built these walls did not use mortar. They treated each stone like a piece of a jigsaw puzzle, fitting it tightly against the others.

 **Page 19** These adobe buildings are in Taos Pueblo, New Mexico. Adobe is made from mud and straw that is mixed together, formed into blocks, and baked in the sun to harden.

 **Page 20** The governor of Maryland lives in this brick home in the state capital, Annapolis. Land for the governor's mansion was bought in the 1850s, and the home was completed twenty years later.

 **Page 21** The Marina City Towers rise up beside the river in Chicago, Illinois. Pie-shaped apartments with wide balconies stack inside each tower. Residents park on the lower levels.

 **Page 22** Architect Robert Bruno created a steel stairway that looks more like a sculpture for his Idaho home.

 **Page 23** An architect from Los Angeles, California, uses a laptop computer. Architects often brainstorm with pencils and tracing paper. When it's time to draw the plans, they use computer-aided-drafting (CAD) programs.

 **Page 24** These carpenters in San Bernardino County, California, frame walls, install windows and doors, and finish the roof.

 **Page 25** This old home is a whaling museum in Point Lobos State Reserve in California. Built in the 1850s by Chinese fishermen, it was also home to Japanese and Portuguese immigrants.

 **Page 26** Children and teachers work together at a day care center in Ann Arbor, Michigan, to paint their new playhouse. What color would you choose?

 **Page 27** Carpenters hammer together a wall frame while it is lying on the floor, then they lift the section and nail it in place. A carpenter's belt holds all the tools he or she needs: hammers, nails, tape measures, pencils, and plumb bobs.

 **Page 28** A Masai woman stands next to the doorway of a home in Africa. The baked mud roof keeps the home cool even on hot days.

 **Page 29** Winters near Karasjok, Norway, are very long and bitterly cold. This log home has thick walls and insulated windows to keep out the cold and hold in the warmth.